FLINT SEPULCHRE

SCULPTURE AND DRAWINGS BY **KEIR SMITH**

Keir Smith has achieved considerable renown as a sculptor of landscape. Usually, such work is sited in landscape and considered in relation to it. Often it is of landscape – constructed from natural materials such as earth and raw fibres. It is unusual to find a sculptor who can evoke the landscape itself through the more orthodox sculptural form of carved objects. To a certain extent, this dominant reading of Smith's work has suppressed more abstract concerns. This exhibition presents an opportunity to assess what will probably be Smith's last 'landscape' and to examine a new direction in his work which betrays the concepts buried in earlier sculpture.

Smith's work is usually sequential, images unfold in a linear fashion, suggesting a journey either through space or time. Topographical and autographical references are integrated into the work and its structure of theme and variations. Keir Smith cites music as one of his most important influences, from the rigorously organised work of Joseph Haydn to the "dazzlingly complex" work of Charles Ives.

The *Flint Sepulchre* series is perhaps more strongly related to Ives than Haydn. Here, rhythm and order are deliberately disturbed and set against each other. Architectural and ecclesiastical images are juxtaposed with attenuated flints. Any narrative connection between the elements is interrupted and meanings are obfuscated.

Smith's interest in space and his more overt engagement with it as tangible matter in the *Flint Sepulchre* series derives from the profound influence of the minimalist sculptors Carl Andre, Robert Smithson and Richard Serra upon his generation of art students. Minimalism might seem an odd background for an artist whose work draws on iconography of familiar forms of found objects and art historical motifs. Yet they are elided with structures which very clearly relate to the minimalist concerns of equality of parts and repetition of forms. Far from presenting a dissonance, this strong sense of structure within beautifully carved forms enforces the potency of Smith's work and endows it with intellectual complexity as much as visual satisfaction.

SARAH SHALGOSKY

CURATOR, MEAD GALLERY

This exhibition represents the conclusion of a long series of works made with railway sleepers and the first showing of a new body of works which have the generic title of *Flint Sepulchre*. Both these series are connected by a long standing interest in landscape, place and architecture. Other works in the exhibition refer to my publicly commissioned works and unrealised projects which deal with related subject matter.

The notion of a journey, often an imaginary one, is implicit in much of the sculpture. The first work to use the journeying notion in a systematic way is the *Iron Road* of 1986, a rather haphazard conglomeration of images cut into the timbers of a railway track, re-laid in the Forest of Dean. Images are part of the track itself, carved into the centre of the sleeper between the cast iron "chairs" which support the rails.

The imagined journeys depicted in later sleeper sculptures often take place along the shore-line. *Iron Band That Binds Green Heart* of 1988 deals with the Cumbrian coastline and *The Dreaming Track*, a closely related work of the same year, is based on my knowledge of the Pembrokeshire coastal path.

Coastal Path, the sleeper set included in this exhibition, was started in 1992 for an exhibition at Rufford Country Park. In 1993 it was completely reworked and augmented, and now appears in its final form. The sculpture continues the maritime connection of other sleeper sets, this time referring to another long distance walking path, the Saxon Shore Way. It proposes a consistent cliffscape containing a single type of building, a lighthouse, in a variety of settings and situations.

The use of repeated imagery in much of my work is extremely important to me and reflects my interest in composers such as Steve Reich and John Adams. Such musical references have always acted as an affirmation of my own concerns.

In *Coastal Path* a landscape fragment is carved in the centre of the sleeper, the marks of the gouge are always evident. Within this landscape a small lighthouse rises, regular, symmetrical and smooth. The lighthouses are made from the same material as the sleeper but are turned and sanded on a lathe, they are made separately and joined to the landscape. *Coastal Path* is one of two late experiments with constructed elements which extend the carved landscape. The other set, *The Fate of Streams*, is sited at the Royal Surrey Hospital in Guildford. Each lighthouse in Coastal Path is set against an incoming wave, but each confrontation in the seven unit set varies considerably; in one sleeper a wave breaks its force against a rocky cliff surmounted by a lighthouse, in another, waves lap gently against a beach where the lighthouse is mounted on a masonry platform.

My subject matter is gathered through what I term "research journeys" where I walk and record images which might be of use with the camera. I have collected thousands of colour slides of landscape, the sea, buildings, sculpture and paintings. These images assimilated during the research journeys are the foundation of all my work.

The Coastal Path derives from two distinct journeys. The first was a trip to Cornwall in the Autumn of 1987 to photograph the tin mine engine houses; this building was later used for the sculptural frieze for Henrietta House, in London. The engine houses were of immediate interest to me because they extended my repertory of buildings associated with the Industrial Revolution, which periodically forms the subject matter of my work. I was struck by the resemblance they bore to the water pumping station near my childhood home in Kent.

On this occasion, I also discovered a lighthouse at the base of a cliff connected to the top by a steep ramp. I always document things that strike an interest but for which I have no immediate plans. A few of these chance findings eventually find their way into a resolved work. Some may even provoke a change of direction in the whole practice. This was the case with the lighthouse which, once gathered, proved to be memorable and was used in designs for a number of unrealised projects towards the end of the 1980s and early 1990s.

The landscape fragments in *Coastal Path*, however, derive from an earlier journey made in the summer of 1987 which had the definite purpose of charting various types of coastal defences that, in turn, related to different historical periods. I started with the immense Roman remains at Richborough, taking in Dover Castle on the way and ended with the World War Two pillboxes which litter the coast of Kent and Sussex. The planned work on coastal defences did not materialise, but the gathered images fed into the Henrietta House project and gradually evolved into *Coastal Path*.

Once the thematic structure of the sleeper set was established I visited other coastal sites to look at particular lighthouses and their geographical context, including trips to Portland Bill and Beachy Head. It was a visit to Dungeness which has two lights, one old and classic the other new, which most determined the pitch of the sculpture. The old Dungeness Light is probably the model for all the buildings in *Coastal Path*. The various lighthouses and locations in *Coastal Path* are not topographically accurate. In fact, local particularities are sometimes deliberately edited out. In the rock strewn peninsular inspired by Portland Bill, for example, the distinctive pyramidical monument to Trinity House, at the edge of the low cliff, has been discarded as a distraction.

To reach its final shape *Coastal Path* was reworked throughout the autumn and winter in 1993. This process has become a consistent feature of my practice, much of my sculpture is worked in phases. Frequently a sculpture is successively exhibited in a modified form. With my earlier carved works, particularly the *Navigator* series of the early 1980s, where images are cut into the salvaged timber of wrecked sailing barges, the motive for reworking was often to refine the carving. I felt the need to eliminate the clumsy handling that resulted from the adoption of a new method of working. My aim is always to define the image more precisely and to disguise the struggle of making. I want my work to appear effortless. I have little interest in the virtuosic, a display of technique for its own sake.

Often the railway carvings are reworked following exposure to the elements in outdoor exhibitions, the surfaces consequently need reviving for the next venue. However, on a more radical level, the exhibited set of carvings may seem incomplete, suggesting an extension. I work in a small studio in London where it is often not possible to see the work in its entirety. I retain this way of working to provide the exhibition with a creative function, that of allowing the sculpture to be seen for the first time.

An exhibition therefore may indicate that a work is to some extent incomplete, a work in progress. *Coastal Path* has been through this process of modification. It was originally made as a five piece set for the exhibition at Rufford Country Park. It was made swiftly, successive images came quickly, there was an element of improvisation about the work.

The reworking has added two units to the set, designed to emphasise the lateral extension of the ensemble, to make it more representative of a journey, to allow the spectator to unfold the work and its meaning gradually, rather than take in the work at a single glance. Each of the lighthouses have been remade, their proportions and relationships to the carved landscapes rethought. The original lighthouses were made of mahogany, the new ones jarrah: the timber of the host sleeper.

Coastal Path is closely related to another much modified sculpture, now entitled *Pier, Ocean and Light*. Originally a very minimal two piece set made for an exhibition at Jesus College Cambridge, the sculpture was extended in 1992. Following my experience working on *Coastal Path* it gained an additional element representing a rocky offshore island surmounted by a lighthouse. The original elements from *Pier, Ocean and Light*, a wave breaking against a decayed break-water and a carving depicting an unfurling wave had, in turn, suggested the basic plan for *Coastal Path*. There is always an element of

cross fertilisation in my work, frequently work on one sculpture reaches an impasse and resolution can only occur following the experience of making another work.

The railway sleeper sets have continued to be made alongside other types of work, usually commissioned, since the late 1980s. Whereas the railway sleeper sets focus on buildings or bridges in a landscape context, much of the other work has isolated architecture as its prime element.

The architectural images are clearly associated with major projects for publicly sited work. Most of these projects remain unrealised, existing only as series of drawings and maquettes. They culminate in the one project brought to completion, the sculptures for Henrietta House in London, entitled *From the Dark Cave*. However, the first project in which architectural images predominate is *The Way of Shadows*, an unrealised work planned in 1989 for the Sustrans Consett to Sunderland sculpture trail. The sculpture was to consist of seven bogie bolster wagons surmounted by steel sculptures depicting a decayed urban site. From this, one recognisable architectural feature arose from the devastated surroundings. The railway trucks were to be sited on a disused railway track which once linked Sunderland and Consett. The entire sculpture was an elegy for the Industrial Revolution, very evidently in a state of atrophy. I was familiar with northern industrial landscapes, and have clear recollections of the noise and energy of the steel mills at Consett.

I intended the *Way of Sorrows* to commemorate a major mining disaster in the nearby pit village of Stanley. The drawings, however, were completed after a journey to Wurtzeburg to study the work of the sixteenth century German sculptor Tilman Riemenschneider as I had become fascinated by German limewood carving. I saw many buildings, particularly the Marienkappelle, originally adorned with Riemenschneider sandstone carvings, which had been reconstructed following heavy Allied bombing during World War Two. The sense of gloom I felt at the destruction of these buildings permeated the drawings for the *Way of Shadows*.

This mood of deep pessimism was not, however, carried over into the following project for Henrietta House, *From the Dark Cave*, although several of the images were derived from the earlier drawings. Images become embedded in the imagination and recur until they are inappropriate or until their power is exhausted.

From the Dark Cave was commissioned by Lynton Plc. via the Public Art Development Trust. It consists of fifteen stone carvings mounted at first floor level on an office development in central London. I worked in close consultation with the architectural firm B.D.P. and the architect Christopher Haddon. It was one of those rare instances where the artist was invited to participate at the design stage rather than when the work is complete and the sculptor is left with a draughty piazza to humanize in some way. This rather exciting collaboration and the sense of purposefulness with which the endeavour proceeded seem to have affected the mood of the work.

The maquettes for *From the Dark Cave* exhibited in this exhibition were used by a small team of stone masons to enlarge and complete the work, and still bear traces of their working life in the dust laden atmosphere of the stone carving sheds. The sculpture is a personalised history of architecture. It continues and expands preoccupations that characterise my previous work, my interest in history, a predisposition to unfold a sequence of images in a linear fashion, and a commitment to subject matter which contains veiled autobiographical references.

In *From the Dark Cave*, successive periods of history are represented by significant buildings, but significant often in terms of their autobiographical resonance. Thus I did not necessarily choose the greatest buildings to denote each historical period, but buildings with which I had personal contact.

The prehistoric age, for example, was represented by Kits Coty House, one of the Medway group of tombs, a local monument, familiar to me since my childhood. Similarly the edifice representing medieval culture was not one of the great Cathedrals, but the remains of St Mary's Abbey, Reculver, dramatically perched on the Kent Coast, another childhood memory. Even those buildings which evoke the twentieth century are in some way personalised images, but in this instance also have claims to being considered great architecture. I used the image of the Senate House of the University of London to announce my admiration for its architect, Charles Holden. I wanted this image to celebrate the collaborations between Holden and Jacob Epstein, whose sculpture is of great interest to me at present. The concluding sculpture of *From the Dark Cave* is a carving of the Canary Wharf Tower which is visible from my front door and back garden.

The long programme of work on the Henrietta House project entailed the setting up of a wood workshop in my studio to attain the required precision for the maquettes which were then enlarged and translated into Portland stone by a small team of masons. For this collaborative process to be successful the maquettes needed to be accurate to pass detailed information on to the carvers when I was not there to supervise the operation, and to ensure that

Maquettes for Henrietta House (From the Dark Cave)   [opposite] Temple at Euston   [above] The Engine House   1991   Brazilian mahogany

the finished sculptures precisely fitted the architectural bays allotted to them on the building. This was the first time that such accuracy was required of my work and the first time that day-to-day modifications, so much a part of my studio approach, were inappropriate. I found working within such tolerances, as well as the collaborative aspects of the work exhilarating, and would work that way again if the opportunity arose.

The architecturally derived images, made with machinery, constructed rather than carved, have been extended into the most recent work, the *Flint Sepulchre* series. The process of constructing sculpture has also prompted me to explore the voids enclosed by the walls of my diminutive buildings, sarcophagi and altars. Carving always seemed to be so much a process of preserving the density of the original block that I have rather neglected interior spaces.

The subject matter of the *Flint Sepulchre* series introduces elements into my sculpture derived from the art and architecture of Italy where I now spend regular periods of research. Despite my longstanding interest in Italian art of the 14th–16th centuries, I first visited the country comparatively recently. Consequently I knew the artworks divorced from their cultural context by isolated examples in museum collections. I became, however, anxious to see such works of art in the settings for which they were conceived. The full meaning of these works can only be adequately unravelled by imaginatively reconstructing the original context. The visual information in an altarpiece is completed and complemented by surrounding frescoes and perhaps a tomb. The subject of an altarpiece or fresco cycle may be related to the legends of the saints to whom the altar or chapel is dedicated while the name of the patron determines the saints who populate the altarpiece.

This richness and complexity of meaning, layer upon layer, is disrupted once the painting enters a museum where it loses its relation to site and to function. To an extent this realisation acted as an affirmation of my desire to make sculpture with multiple layers of meaning which can only be unravelled gradually.

In the railway sleeper series there was a desire to unify the structure and present a coherent unfolding sequence of images. In the *Flint Sepulchre* series there is a reluctance to rely on such order, disparate objects are thrust together and meanings are provisional and confused. This strategy is deliberate and seems to reflect not only the complexity of the visual and cultural material from which the sculptures derive but acknowledges my profound interest in the dazzlingly complex and heterogeneous music of Charles Ives.

Typically, the *Flint Sepulchre* sculptures juxtapose architectural or ecclesiastical elements such as painted altarpieces, sarcophagi, or even the altars themselves with irregular carved objects deriving from the form of flints. The ecclesiastical objects are diminutive, the flints vastly over-sized. The flints, which are often stretched in form, are made from jarrah. The symmetrical, geometric ecclesiastical objects are made from mahogany, often with jarrah inserts. Like the lighthouses in *Coastal Path*, the *Flint Sepulchre* sculptures force the machine made and the hand crafted together.

The ecclesiastical images, while reflecting my interest in Italy, do not chart a straightforward love story. To some extent the Italian themes explore feelings of disquiet. One group of images derive from a research journey to Padua in 1992 to see, amongst other things the remains of the Mantegna frescos in the Cappella Ovetari, Chiesa degli Eremitani. These paintings consist of a jigsaw of fragments, the cycle being largely destroyed as a result of Allied bombing in World War Two. In the church I saw a photograph of the devastated building following the raid. It showed a chapel to the left of the High Altar, the roof burned away and open to the sky with an immense shattered wooden beam leaning against a 14th century fresco cycle.

This image has haunted me but has not emerged in a resolved sculpture. I sometimes find certain themes too powerful to deal with. Plans to work with the subject of the wrecked church, investigated in sketchbooks and rough maquettes, came to nothing. The literalness of my use of the image failed to digest its essential nature and resulted in something akin to an illustration rather than a work that embodied the significance of the event. I suspect that the photograph underlies much of the thinking which informs the *Flint Sepulchre* series; a sinister undercurrent beneath a celebratory surface.

This series of sculptures charts my rather complex feelings towards Italy, where despite my love of the art, I am essentially an alien, and can only remain so as an unbeliever in a Catholic country. The element of the exotic and strange is deeply important and the sense of cultural dislocation I feel somehow augments my dismay at the destruction wrought by warfare, in which I have a vague feeling of complicity.

The Italian images are usually gathered by the camera as a result of a direct confrontation with the object, the sarcophagi from the Camposanto in Pisa for example, but increasingly they may be culled from paintings, the empty sarcophagus, of course, occurs in countless depictions of the resurrection of Christ or the Assumption of the Virgin.

The extended flints which separate the regular, architecturally derived images in the *Flint Sepulchre* series were suggested by a group of my early works, the *Flint Axe* set, which were shown at the AIR Gallery in London in 1979. These installations explored, in a quasi-archaeological fashion, the way that flint axes had been instrumental in allowing forests to be felled to enable the development of a stable culture based on agriculture. The exhibition represented a prehistoric panorama of the landscape.

The landscape and architecture of Kent and indeed South Eastern England, the main area of my image gathering walks, is dominated by flint, the main building material of the region. Most 14th century churches are made from either undressed or knapped flints. Flints continue to fascinate me. Now it is not their archaeological significance which interests me but the irregularity and unpredictability of their form.

In the linear sequences of images which characterise sculptures from the *Flint Sepulchre* series, the stretched flints tend to break up, interrupt, disrupt or subvert any developing narrative connection between the architectural and ecclesiastical objects. The effect intended is not quite chaotic, but meaning must be fought for or deduced rather than taken for granted. Later "flints" in the series have become even more extended and exaggerated. They even seem to contain parody elements referring to the flint and bone sculptures of Henry Moore and the pierced organic forms of Barbara Hepworth. In opposition to the ecclesiastical elements, the stretched flints act as a sort of visual cadenza while the more geometric, architectural components form a secure structural base.

In *The Eye of the Needle*, made from three elements, a long winding form, pierced at one end, barely retains a vestigial trace of the flint gathered on the South Coast, near Beachy Head, that inspired it. This low lying form separates a monumental pillar from a casket-like object, reminiscent of an altar or sarcophagus. The pillar, distantly based on Wren's monument to the Great Fire of London, is surmounted by a lighthouse on a rocky promontory. This lighthouse memorial forms a bridge between the railway sleeper carvings and the rest of the *Flint Sepulchre* series. The form at the top of the monument was the last element to be decided, it was made at the same time as work on *Coastal Path* was being concluded.

KEIR SMITH   1993

Eye of the Needle 1993 Brazilian mahogany and jarrah

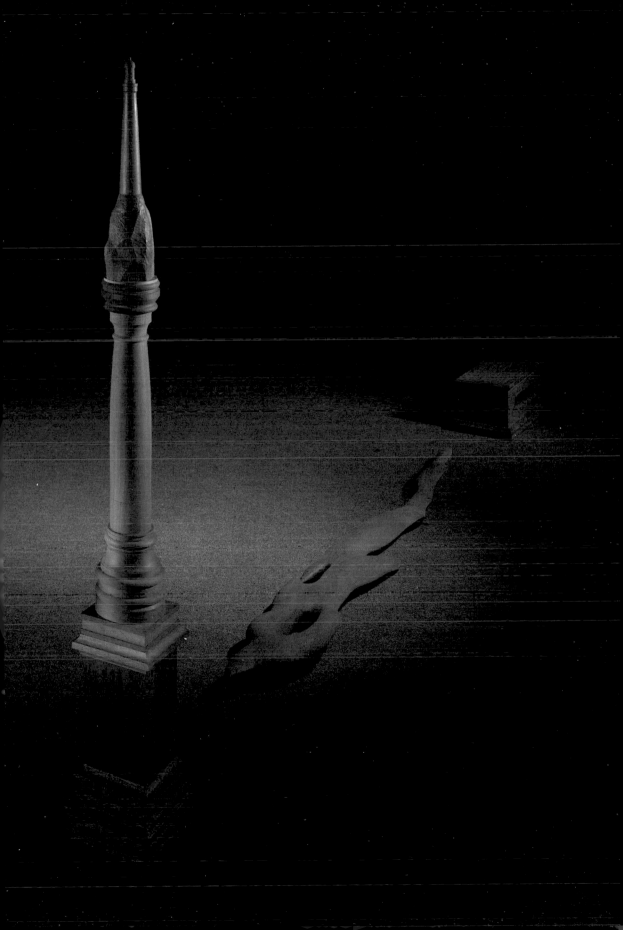

KEIR SMITH

Born in Kent 1950. Lives in London

1969–73   Department of Fine Art, University of Newcastle upon Tyne

1973–75   Chelsea School of Art Postgraduate Degree

Currently Principal Lecturer: Subject Leader in Sculpture, Wimbledon School of Art

SELECTED SITED SCULPTURE

1985–86   *Windborn : The Phoenix*, Garden Festival, Stoke on Trent

1986   *The Iron Road*, Forest of Dean

1986   *Topsail*, Baltic Wharf, Bristol

1990   *The Way of Clouds*, Usher Gallery, Lincoln

1992   *From the Dark Cave*, Henrietta House, London

ONE PERSON EXHIBITIONS

1977   *Flint Axe*, Hays Gallery, Sheffield

1977   *Mark/Meaning*, A.I.R. Gallery, London

1979   *Speculations*, Hatton Gallery Newcastle upon Tyne

1980   *Like Nimrod's Tower*, Acme Gallery, London

1981   *Ceres*, Spectro Gallery, Newcastle upon Tyne

1982   *Sailing Ancient Seas*, Ceolfrith Gallery, Sunderland and Ikon Gallery, Birmingham

1983   *The Coniston Variations*, Demarco Gallery, Edinburgh

1984–85   *Navigator*, Rochdale Art Gallery and national tour

1985   *Towards the Iron Road*, Bluecoat Gallery, Liverpool

1986   *The Dust of Learning*, Artsite Gallery, Bath

1987   *Project Drawings 1983–1987*, Posterngate Gallery, Hull

1989   *The Dreaming Track*, Laing Art Gallery, Newcastle upon Tyne and Wolverhampton Art Gallery

1992   *Coastal Path*, Rufford Country Park

1994   *Flint Sepulchre*, Mead Gallery, Bury St Edmunds Art Gallery and tour

Maquettes for Henrietta House (From the Dark Cave)
1991
Brazilian mahogany

Coastal Path
1993
Jarrah

Eye of the Needle
1993
Brazilian mahogany and jarrah

Castelfranco High Chair
1994
Brazilian mahogany and jarrah

Domenico's House
1994
Brazilian mahogany and jarrah

Dreaming Assisi
(Drawings for an unrealised project)
1991
Watercolour on paper

The Fate of Streams
1991
Ink wash and watercolour on paper

The Way of Shadows
1991
Ink wash on paper

FLINT SEPULCHRE

SCULPTURE AND DRAWINGS BY

KEIR SMITH

19 February – 19 March 1994

Mead Gallery, Arts Centre, University of Warwick
Coventry CV4 7AL

Exhibition organised and toured by
the Mead Gallery

ACKNOWLEDGEMENT

We would like to thank
the Wimbledon School of Art Research Committee
for its support of this exhibition

ISBN 0 902683 20 9

Published by

the University of Warwick

Photographs

Ben Johnson, Keir Smith & Alan Watson

Design & production

Peter McGrath, Groundwork, Skipton

Printed in Great Britain

UNIVERSITY OF WARWICK

Supported by the
Wimbledon School of Art
Research Committee